DENIM NIKALLAIAS HO

Feeling Like a Fraud

*How Gay Men Can Break Free from Imposter Syndrome
and Live Authentically*

Contents

Introduction: Why You Feel Like a Fraud—And Why It's Not Your Fault

If you've ever felt like you're living a double life, pretending to be someone you're not, or waiting for the moment everyone figures out you don't belong, you're not alone. For gay men, this feeling has a name: imposter syndrome. It's that voice in your head whispering, *"You're not good enough, smart enough, talented enough. You don't deserve this."*

But let's get something straight: you didn't create that voice. It was planted there, rooted in the world we grew up in—a world that taught us to shrink, hide, and question our worth.

Why Do So Many Gay Men Struggle With Imposter Syndrome?

For starters, think about what it's like to grow up gay in a society built on heteronormativity. From a young age, we're bombarded with messages about what it means to be "normal." Boys are supposed to like girls. Men are supposed to act tough, show no emotion, and follow a straight (pun intended) path toward marriage, kids, and a white picket fence.

When you don't fit into that mold, you start to internalize the idea that there's something wrong with you. Even if you had supportive family and friends, the pressure to conform is everywhere. And that pressure doesn't just make you feel different—it can make you feel like you'll never measure up.

The Roots of "Not Enoughness"

Let's talk about this idea of "not enoughness." Where does it even come from? Society teaches us that our worth is tied to things like success, masculinity, and how well we can fit into roles designed for straight people. When you grow up feeling like you have to prove yourself—to your family, your peers, or even yourself—you carry that "not enough" baggage into adulthood.

And here's the kicker: even when you achieve success, that little voice doesn't go away. It just changes its tune. Instead of saying, *"You'll never make it,"* it starts saying, *"You don't deserve this."*

Identity, Shame, and Success

For gay men, success can feel complicated. On the one hand, we often overcompensate to prove we belong—working harder, achieving more, and aiming for perfection. On the other hand, success can trigger feelings of shame.

Why? Because deep down, a part of us might still believe we're unworthy. That shame becomes a weight we carry, holding us back from fully embracing our achievements, our identity, and even our relationships.

The Cost of Shrinking Ourselves

When we feel like frauds, we start to shrink ourselves—hiding parts of who we are to avoid judgment or rejection. We say yes when we mean no. We avoid risks because we're afraid of failing. We downplay our strengths because we don't want to seem arrogant.

But here's the thing: shrinking doesn't protect you. It limits you. It keeps you stuck in a cycle of self-doubt, anxiety, and burnout.

The Emotional and Relational Toll

The emotional toll of imposter syndrome is no joke. It shows up as anxiety that never lets you rest, self-doubt that makes you question every decision, and burnout that leaves you feeling empty—even when you're outwardly "successful."

And it doesn't just affect you; it impacts your relationships, too. Maybe you struggle with intimacy because you're afraid people will see the "real you." Maybe you overgive in relationships, falling into codependency or people-pleasing. Or maybe you've built walls so high that nobody can get close to you—not even the people who truly care.

Missing Out on Authenticity

When you spend your life trying to prove you're enough, you miss out on the chance to just *be*. To express yourself fully. To connect with others authentically. To live a life that feels true to who you are—not who you think you're supposed to be.

The Promise of Living Authentically

But here's the good news: it doesn't have to be this way. Living authentically—unapologetically, even—is possible. It's about embracing who you are, flaws and all, and letting go of the need to prove your worth to anyone, including yourself.

When you step into your truth, you discover a freedom you've never known. A freedom to take up space. To love and be loved. To chase your dreams without fear of failure.

How This Book Will Help

This book is your guide to breaking free from imposter syndrome and living authentically as a gay man. Together, we'll unpack where these feelings come from, how they show up in your life, and most importantly, how to overcome them.

You'll learn practical tools, and gain insights that will help you stop feeling like a fraud and start living the life you deserve.

Because here's the truth: You *are* enough. You always have been. And it's time to start believing it.

Chapter 1: Understanding the Fraud Mindset

What Is Imposter Syndrome?

At its core, imposter syndrome is the belief that you're not as competent, capable, or worthy as others think you are. It's the feeling that your success is a fluke, your achievements don't count, and sooner or later, someone's going to find out you're just faking it.

Psychologists first defined imposter syndrome in the late 1970s as a pattern of self-doubt and fear of being exposed as a fraud. But here's the thing: it's not officially recognized as a mental health diagnosis. It's more like a psychological experience—a mix of self-doubt, anxiety, and insecurity that can creep into every area of your life.

Symptoms of Imposter Syndrome

Imposter syndrome shows up in different ways, but here are some common signs:

- **Perfectionism:** You set impossibly high standards for yourself and beat yourself up when you don't meet them.

- **Fear of Failure:** You avoid risks because failing feels like confirmation that you're not good enough.
- **Overworking:** You work twice as hard as everyone else to "prove" you belong.
- **Downplaying Success:** You brush off your achievements, saying things like, "I just got lucky" or "It wasn't a big deal."
- **Fear of Exposure:** You're constantly worried that someone will figure out you don't belong.

Sound familiar? For many of us, these feelings aren't just occasional—they're woven into how we see ourselves.

How It Manifests in LGBTQ+ Communities

Now, let's talk about how imposter syndrome shows up for LGBTQ+ people, especially gay men. While anyone can experience it, there's something unique about how it plays out when your identity has been marginalized.

For gay men, imposter syndrome is often tied to our experiences of coming out, hiding parts of ourselves, and navigating a world that doesn't always accept us. Think about it:

- You've been told, directly or indirectly, that who you are is "wrong" or "less than."
- You've had to perform versions of yourself—acting straighter, tougher, or more palatable—to fit in.
- You've internalized the idea that your worth is conditional, based on how well you conform to expectations.

These experiences create a perfect storm for imposter syndrome.

It's not just about doubting your skills; it's about doubting your very right to take up space.

The Role of Internalized Oppression

A big piece of this puzzle is **internalized oppression**. This happens when societal messages about LGBTQ+ people—like being "less masculine" or "not normal"—become part of your own thinking. Even if you know those messages are wrong, they can leave scars that affect how you see yourself.

For example:

- **Internalized Shame:** You might feel like you need to prove you're "good enough" to compensate for being gay.
- **Overcompensation:** Maybe you overachieve at work or in your personal life because deep down, you feel like you're starting from a deficit.
- **Fear of Visibility:** You might avoid being too outspoken or too authentic, worried it will confirm stereotypes or make you a target for criticism.

When you carry this kind of baggage, it's easy to feel like a fraud—like no matter how much you do, you'll never measure up.

Imposter syndrome is tough for anyone, but for gay men and others in the LGBTQ+ community, it's layered with the weight of systemic oppression, societal rejection, and the pressure to succeed in a world that hasn't always been kind to us. The good news? These feelings are not permanent, and they're not a reflection of your true worth. The first step to breaking free is understanding where they come from—and realizing they don't have to define you.

Where Does It Come From?

If you've ever wondered why imposter syndrome feels like it's etched into your brain, the answer often lies in your past. Like so many of our struggles, it starts young—shaped by our earliest experiences, the world around us, and the people closest to us.

Early Childhood: Fitting In vs. Standing Out

From the moment we're old enough to understand the world, we're also old enough to feel the pressure to *fit in*. For most kids, standing out is a risk—they know that being "different" can make you a target. For queer kids, this pressure is magnified because *who we are* is often what makes us stand out.

Think about it:

- Maybe you realized early on that you didn't quite fit the mold of what a "real boy" was supposed to be.
- Maybe you liked the "wrong" things, acted the "wrong" way, or had feelings you didn't fully understand yet.

When you grow up feeling like you have to hide or downplay parts of yourself, you start to question your authenticity. Over time, this can create a pattern of self-doubt: *If people knew the real me, would they still accept me?*

The Power of Societal Messaging

Even if your family or close friends were accepting, the larger world had its own messages about who you were "allowed" to be. These messages come from everywhere—TV shows, movies, social media, schools, religion, and culture.

For gay men, these messages can be toxic. We're often portrayed as stereotypes—comic relief, sidekicks, or overly sexualized characters. Rarely do we see gay men as heroes, leaders, or complex people with full lives. And when we *are* shown in a positive light, it's often tied to perfection: the impossibly fit, wildly successful, always put-together guy.

What does this teach us? That our worth isn't inherent— it's conditional. If you want respect, you better earn it by being exceptional. Anything less, and you risk being dismissed, ridiculed, or forgotten.

Familial Expectations: The Fraud Narrative at Home

Now let's bring it closer to home. For many of us, our families were the first to set the bar for what was expected of us. These expectations can feel even heavier if you grew up with parents who wanted you to embody a certain kind of success—academic, professional, or social.

For gay men, familial expectations often come with an added layer of tension:

- **Hiding Parts of Yourself:** If your family wasn't fully accepting, you may have felt the need to hide or downplay your sexuality to gain their approval. This can create a deep-rooted belief that you have to "perform" to be loved.
- **Overcompensating:** Even in supportive families, many gay men feel pressure to "make up" for their identity by excelling in other areas. You might think, *If I can't give them*

the life they expected, at least I can make them proud in other ways.

- **Seeking Validation:** If your family's approval was conditional, you might find yourself constantly striving for external validation as an adult—because deep down, you're not sure if your worth is enough on its own.

When you add all of this together—early feelings of not fitting in, societal pressures to be perfect, and familial expectations—you start to see how imposter syndrome takes root. It's not just about doubting your skills or achievements. It's about years of internalizing the message that who you are is somehow not enough.

But here's the truth: these messages are lies. They come from a world that didn't know how to see your worth, not from anything lacking within you. And the sooner you unpack where these feelings come from, the sooner you can start rewriting the narrative of your life.

The Cost of Living Small

Living small might feel safe—it's easier to stay quiet, blend in, and avoid drawing attention to yourself. But in reality, it comes with a heavy price. When we hold ourselves back, hide who we are, or constantly question our worth, we lose so much more than we gain.

Missed Opportunities for Growth and Leadership

Think about the times you've hesitated to step up. Maybe you passed on a promotion because you didn't feel "ready." Maybe you stayed silent in a meeting, convinced your ideas weren't good enough. Maybe you avoided a big, bold dream because the thought of failing felt unbearable.

When imposter syndrome keeps you playing small, you miss out on moments to grow. Leadership isn't about being perfect; it's about showing up, being vulnerable, and taking risks. But if you're constantly questioning your worth, it's hard to take those chances.

Missed opportunities don't just hold you back professionally—they limit your ability to contribute your unique voice and perspective. The world *needs* people like you to step into leadership roles, to create change, and to inspire others. When you stay small, you rob both yourself and the world of that possibility.

Emotional Exhaustion from Masking and Performing

Living small often comes with a side hustle no one talks about: the endless job of masking and performing. If you've spent years trying to "fit in," you know how exhausting it can be.

You monitor how you speak, dress, or act. You downplay your accomplishments to avoid seeming arrogant or attracting too much attention. You pretend everything's fine, even when you're overwhelmed, because showing vulnerability feels like a risk.

This kind of constant self-monitoring drains your energy. It leaves you emotionally depleted, with little left for the things that truly matter. Over time, masking and performing can lead to burnout—not just at work, but in your relationships and personal life, too.

Disconnection from Your Authentic Self and Values

Perhaps the most heartbreaking cost of living small is the distance it creates between you and your authentic self. When you're so busy trying to be who you think the world wants you to be, you lose touch with who you really are.

Living authentically means aligning your life with your values, passions, and true desires. But when you're stuck in a cycle of self-doubt and fear, those things can feel out of reach. Instead of pursuing what lights you up, you settle for what feels safe. Instead of embracing your quirks and unique traits, you try to smooth them out.

This disconnection doesn't just affect you—it also impacts your relationships. When you're not living authentically, it's hard to form deep, meaningful connections with others. You might attract people who only know the "safe" version of you, leaving you feeling unseen and misunderstood.

Living small might feel like self-protection, but it's actually self-sabotage. The opportunities you miss, the energy you lose, and the distance you create from your true self aren't worth the illusion of safety.

The good news is, it's never too late to stop shrinking. You have the power to reclaim your energy, reconnect with your authentic self, and step into a life that feels bigger, bolder, and more aligned with who you are. All it takes is the courage to stop living small and start showing up as your full, unapologetic self.

Chapter 2: The Roots of Shrinking

Cultural and Societal Pressures

For gay men, the pressure to live up to societal expectations isn't just about fitting in—it's about survival. Whether consciously or unconsciously, many of us grow up believing that the world will only accept us under certain conditions. These conditions shape how we see ourselves, how we show up, and how we navigate life.

The Myth of the "Acceptable Gay"
Society often sends a clear message: *If you want to be accepted, you have to be the right kind of gay.* This myth of the "acceptable gay" demands that we be palatable, non-threatening, and quiet. What does this look like in real life?

- You're expected to dress well and be charming but never too flamboyant.
- You can be in a relationship, but it shouldn't be too "public" or "political."
- You're allowed to succeed, but you better not make anyone

uncomfortable by being too bold or outspoken.

This myth pressures us to erase the parts of ourselves that don't fit into a narrow, sanitized version of gayness—one that's designed to make straight people comfortable. It's not about authenticity; it's about conformity. And the worst part? Many of us internalize this standard and begin holding ourselves to it, often without even realizing it.

Perfectionism as a Shield Against Judgment

One of the ways we cope with this pressure is through perfectionism. The logic goes like this: *If I can be flawless—at work, in my relationships, in how I present myself—then maybe they'll accept me.*

Perfectionism becomes a shield, a way to protect ourselves from criticism and judgment. But the cost is high. Striving for perfection means constantly second-guessing yourself, obsessing over details, and setting impossible standards.

And the truth is, even when you achieve "perfection," it rarely feels like enough. That little voice in your head keeps saying, *What if they still don't accept you?* Or worse, *What if they find a flaw and reject you completely?*

Navigating Intersectional Identities in a Heteronormative World

For those of us who carry additional marginalized identities—such as being a person of color, coming from an immigrant background, or living with a disability—the pressure becomes even more complicated. Intersectionality means we're navigating multiple layers of identity in a world that wasn't built to accommodate any of them.

In a heteronormative world:

- **You might feel the need to "code-switch,"** adapting your behavior or appearance to fit into different spaces.
- **You might face unique stereotypes,** like being seen as hypersexual, overly effeminate, or "exotic."
- **You might feel torn between communities,** worrying that you're "not gay enough" for LGBTQ+ spaces or "too gay" for cultural or familial ones.

These overlapping pressures make it even harder to embrace your authenticity. It's like trying to navigate a maze where the rules keep changing depending on who's watching.

Cultural and societal pressures don't just ask us to blend in—they demand that we shrink ourselves to fit into molds we didn't create. The myth of the "acceptable gay" and the burden of perfectionism may feel protective, but in reality, they're prisons. Breaking free means rejecting these impossible standards and embracing the full, messy, beautiful truth of who you are. Because you don't need to be perfect to be worthy. You already are.

The Fear of Rejection

Rejection is one of the most painful experiences we face as human beings. For gay men, this fear often runs deeper, shaped by a lifetime of messages—both spoken and unspoken—that who we are might not be acceptable. Whether it's fear of being judged, excluded, or outright attacked, this fear pushes many of us to play small.

Why Being "Too Much" Feels Dangerous

For many gay men, there's an unspoken rule we internalize early on: *Don't be too much.* Too loud. Too flamboyant. Too opinionated. Too vulnerable. The idea is that if you tone yourself down, you're less likely to draw attention—and less likely to be rejected.

This fear is rooted in survival. When you've been mocked, criticized, or alienated for being yourself, it makes sense to avoid anything that might trigger those experiences again. But over time, this can turn into self-policing. You second-guess your every move, wondering: *Am I being too much right now? Am I making people uncomfortable?*

The result? You hold back your brilliance, your quirks, and your voice—anything that might make you stand out. But living this way is suffocating. It creates a version of you that feels watered down, disconnected from your true self.

The Trauma Response of Shrinking or Staying Silent

This fear of rejection isn't just in your head; it's deeply connected to your nervous system. When faced with situations where rejection feels likely, your body goes into a trauma response—fight, flight, freeze, or fawn. For many gay men, the response often looks like shrinking or staying silent.

- **Shrinking:** You minimize yourself to avoid being noticed or criticized. You might avoid speaking up, sharing your opinions, or taking up space.

- **Staying Silent:** You hold back your truth, whether that's an idea at work, an emotion in a relationship, or even your authentic identity in certain spaces.

These responses are your body's way of keeping you safe, but they come at a cost. Shrinking and staying silent might protect you in the moment, but they reinforce the belief that your full self is dangerous, unworthy, or unlovable.

Releasing the Need for Universal Approval

Here's a hard truth: No matter how much you shrink, silence yourself, or strive for perfection, rejection is still a possibility. You can't control how others perceive you, and you'll never be everyone's cup of tea. But here's the good news: *You don't have to be.*

Releasing the need for universal approval is one of the most liberating things you can do. It means recognizing that other people's opinions don't define your worth. It means giving yourself permission to be disliked—because the people who matter will love you for exactly who you are.

When you stop chasing approval, you make room for something much more valuable: self-acceptance. You begin to see that the right people, opportunities, and experiences will find you when you show up authentically. And the ones that fall away? They were never meant for you anyway.

The fear of rejection is powerful, but it doesn't have to control your life. By understanding where this fear comes from and learning to let go of the need for approval, you can start to step into your truth—unapologetically, without shrinking, and without fear of being "too much." Because the right people will never ask you to be less.

The Quest for External Validation

Let's be real: who doesn't enjoy a little praise? Compliments, recognition, and applause feel great—they light us up, boost our confidence, and make us feel seen. But for many gay men, external validation becomes more than a bonus—it turns into the *only* way we measure our self-worth.

The Dopamine Cycle of Seeking Praise and Recognition
Here's how it works: every time someone praises you, your brain gives you a hit of dopamine, the "feel-good" chemical. It's like a reward system, reinforcing the idea that external validation equals value.

- You excel at work, and your boss praises you—dopamine hit.
- You post a perfectly curated photo online, and the likes pour in—dopamine hit.
- You play the role of the funny, agreeable friend at a party, and everyone loves you—dopamine hit.

These moments feel incredible, but they're also addictive. The more validation you receive, the more you crave it. Over time, your brain starts to prioritize those external rewards over your internal sense of self-worth. You're not just looking for validation—you're depending on it to feel okay about yourself.

The Fragility of Basing Self-Worth on Others' Opinions
The problem with relying on external validation is that it's

fragile. What happens when the applause stops? When the compliments fade? When someone criticizes you or doesn't give you the recognition you were hoping for?

Basing your self-worth on others' opinions is like building a house on quicksand. It's unstable, unpredictable, and constantly shifting. One negative comment can undo ten compliments. One moment of being overlooked can make you question your entire value.

When you tie your sense of worth to what others think, you give them control over how you feel about yourself. And the truth is, other people's opinions are often about *them*—their biases, moods, and perspectives—not about you.

Reclaiming Your Inner Authority

The key to breaking free from this cycle is learning to validate yourself. This means reclaiming your inner authority and becoming the ultimate source of your own worth.

- **Celebrate Your Wins:** You don't need someone else to tell you you've done a good job. Take a moment to acknowledge your efforts and achievements, no matter how small they may seem.
- **Define Your Values:** What truly matters to *you*? When you live in alignment with your values, you start to measure success by your own standards, not someone else's.
- **Practice Self-Compassion:** Be kind to yourself, especially in moments of failure or rejection. Remind yourself that your worth isn't tied to perfection or performance—it's inherent.

When you learn to validate yourself, you become less dependent on external praise. The dopamine cycle loses its grip, and your sense of self becomes rooted in something unshakable: your own inner truth.

The quest for external validation is a natural response to growing up in a world that often told us we weren't enough. But chasing praise and approval will never fill the void. True validation comes from within—from recognizing your own worth, owning your brilliance, and refusing to let anyone else define your value. You've always had the power to give yourself the validation you deserve. Now's the time to claim it.

Chapter 3: Recognizing the Masks You Wear

How We Mask Our True Selves

For many gay men, the instinct to mask who we really are feels almost second nature. It's a survival mechanism—a way to navigate a world that hasn't always been kind to difference. But while masking may protect us in the moment, it often leaves us feeling disconnected, exhausted, and invisible. Let's break down the ways we hide and why it's time to stop.

The Chameleon Effect: Blending In to Survive

From a young age, many of us learn to adapt to the expectations of those around us. We become social chameleons, blending in to avoid standing out. This might mean:

- **Adopting behaviors that feel safer:** Lowering your voice, dressing more conservatively, or avoiding certain topics in conversation.
- **Echoing others' opinions:** Agreeing with the majority to avoid conflict, even if it doesn't align with what you really

think.

- **Suppressing your true feelings:** Laughing off offensive comments or staying quiet when something bothers you.

The chameleon effect is rooted in self-protection. When you've faced judgment, bullying, or rejection, blending in feels like a way to shield yourself. But over time, this constant adapting can make you feel like you've lost touch with who you are.

Overcompensating with Humor, Intellect, or Charm

For some of us, masking doesn't mean blending in—it means standing out in carefully curated ways. We lean on tools like humor, intellect, or charm to distract from parts of ourselves we feel insecure about.

- **Humor:** You become the funny guy, cracking jokes to keep the mood light. It's easier to make people laugh than to let them see your vulnerability.
- **Intellect:** You dazzle others with your knowledge, ensuring you're respected for your brains while keeping your emotions off-limits.
- **Charm:** You master the art of being liked, becoming the perfect host, friend, or coworker to ensure you're indispensable.

These strategies often work—they win approval and make us feel valued. But they also come at a cost. When you overcompensate, you're showing people a version of yourself, not the real you. It's like wearing a mask that hides your depth, your struggles, and your full humanity.

Hyper-Achievement as a Defense Mechanism

Another common way we mask is by striving for hyper-achievement. This is the "If I can just be the best, they can't criticize me" mindset.

- You overwork yourself to excel in your career, believing success will shield you from judgment.
- You obsess over fitness or appearance, hoping perfection will make you untouchable.
- You pursue one milestone after another, thinking each accomplishment will finally prove your worth.

While achievement can be fulfilling, hyper-achievement is rooted in fear. It's not about genuine growth; it's about building a fortress around yourself. The problem is, no amount of success can protect you from self-doubt or make you feel truly seen.

The Cost of Masking

Each of these strategies—blending in, overcompensating, or overachieving—might feel like armor, but it's armor that weighs you down. It keeps people from knowing the real you and, more importantly, keeps *you* from knowing the real you.

The truth is, you don't need to hide, perform, or prove your worth. The parts of yourself you've been masking—your quirks, emotions, and unique perspective—are the very things that make you extraordinary.

Stepping out from behind the mask takes courage, but it's the first step toward living authentically. And when you do, you'll discover something powerful: the people and opportunities that are meant for you will embrace you exactly as you are. No performance required.

The Toll of Inauthenticity

Masking your true self may feel like a way to protect yourself from judgment, rejection, or misunderstanding, but over time, it takes a significant toll. The price of inauthenticity shows up in every corner of your life, leaving you drained, isolated, and disconnected.

Emotional Burnout and Cognitive Dissonance

Living inauthentically requires constant effort. You're always on alert, monitoring how you talk, act, and show up in different situations. This emotional labor adds up, leading to burnout.

- **Emotional burnout:** You might feel exhausted, unmotivated, or even resentful without knowing why. It's the cost of holding back your real self while projecting a carefully managed version of you to the world.
- **Cognitive dissonance:** This is the mental stress of living out of alignment with your truth. On one hand, you want to be authentic, but on the other, you feel pressure to conform or please others. This inner conflict creates a persistent sense of unease or dissatisfaction, as if you're always at odds with yourself.

Burnout and dissonance don't just drain your energy—they also rob you of the joy and freedom that come with living authentically.

The Loneliness of Hiding Who You Are

Hiding parts of yourself might keep you safe from judgment, but it also isolates you. When you're constantly masking, it can feel like no one truly knows or understands you.

Even if you're surrounded by people, you might feel alone because:

- You're not showing them the real you.
- You wonder if they'd still accept you if they knew the truth.
- You feel like an outsider in your own life, disconnected from the relationships that are supposed to bring you comfort.

This loneliness can be especially painful in LGBTQ+ communities, where many of us long for connection and belonging. But true connection isn't possible when you're hiding behind a mask.

How Masking Sabotages Deep Relationships

Authentic relationships require vulnerability. They're built on honesty, trust, and mutual understanding. But when you're masking, you're holding back parts of yourself, making it difficult to build these foundations.

Masking can show up in relationships as:

- **People-pleasing:** Always agreeing or going along with others to avoid conflict, even when it goes against your values or needs.
- **Emotional distance:** Avoiding deeper conversations or hiding your struggles because you're afraid of being judged or rejected.
- **Superficial connections:** Forming relationships where people only know the "safe" version of you, leaving you feeling unseen and misunderstood.

While masking may feel like a way to maintain relationships, it actually undermines them. It prevents you from being fully present, fully known, and fully loved.

Reclaiming Your Authenticity

The toll of inauthenticity is steep, but it's never too late to change. The first step is acknowledging the cost—burnout, loneliness, and shallow relationships—and recognizing that you deserve better.

Living authentically isn't easy, but it's the only way to find true connection, fulfillment, and peace. When you stop hiding, you give yourself permission to be seen, valued, and loved for who you truly are. And that's a gift no mask can ever provide.

Unveiling the Masks

Living authentically starts with an honest look at where you've been hiding. It's not always easy to admit when you're not being real, but it's the first step toward reclaiming your truth. Think of this process as gently peeling back layers, one by one, to uncover the you that's been waiting underneath.

Practical Exercises to Identify Where You're Not Being Real

Sometimes, we don't even realize where we're masking. These exercises can help you pinpoint areas in your life where you're not showing up authentically:

- **Life Audit:** Take a sheet of paper and divide it into three columns:

- **Where am I fully myself?** Write down spaces, relationships, or activities where you feel free to be you.
- **Where am I holding back?** Note situations where you find yourself censoring or adapting.
- **What triggers my need to mask?** Identify patterns— specific people, environments, or topics that make you feel like you can't show up authentically.
- **Energy Check-In:** Pay attention to how you feel after social interactions or workdays. Do you feel energized or drained? If it's the latter, consider whether masking or overcompensating played a role.
- **Feedback Loop:** Ask a trusted friend or loved one, "When do you think I'm most myself? Are there times when I seem to hold back?" Sometimes, others can see patterns we miss.

Journaling Prompts to Uncover Hidden Fears and Motivations
Journaling can be a powerful tool for self-discovery. Use these prompts to dig deeper into what's driving your need to mask:

1. What are three things I'm afraid people will think if they see the real me?
2. Where did I learn that parts of myself weren't acceptable? Who or what taught me that?
3. What would I gain by being fully authentic in my relation- ships? What might I lose?
4. Who inspires me to be more myself, and why?
5. What's one part of myself I've been hiding that I'm ready to start showing?

As you write, try not to judge yourself. The goal isn't to "fix" anything; it's to understand where these fears and motivations come from so you can address them with compassion.

Strategies to Start Peeling Back the Layers

Once you've identified where you're masking and why, the next step is to take action. These strategies can help you begin showing up more authentically:

1. **Start Small:** Choose one area of your life where you feel safest experimenting with authenticity. This might be with a close friend, a supportive coworker, or even just in how you express yourself on social media.
2. **Practice Saying "No" or "Yes" Authentically:** If you've been a people-pleaser, try saying "no" to something you don't want to do. If you've held back from opportunities out of fear, say "yes" to something that excites you.
3. **Share a Truth:** Open up about something real—an opinion, a story, or a feeling—with someone you trust. Notice how it feels to be seen in your truth, even if it's a little scary.
4. **Affirm Yourself Daily:** Each day, write down one thing you like about yourself—something unrelated to external validation. This helps you build an internal foundation of self-worth, making it easier to show up authentically.
5. **Celebrate Progress:** Each time you make a choice to be more real, celebrate it! Authenticity isn't an all-or-nothing game—it's a journey. Every step counts.

Unveiling the masks isn't about ripping them off all at once—it's about creating space to explore who you are beneath them. The process may feel vulnerable, but it's also freeing. As you peel back the layers, you'll begin to experience the joy and connection that comes with being fully seen and fully yourself. And once you've tasted that freedom, you won't want to live any other way.

Chapter 4: Reclaiming Your Worth

Reframing Your Narrative

The stories we tell ourselves shape how we see the world—and how we see ourselves. For many gay men, those stories have been influenced by years of societal conditioning, rejection, or shame. But here's the good news: just because you've been carrying a certain narrative doesn't mean you're stuck with it. You have the power to rewrite your story into one that reflects your truth, your strength, and your inherent worth.

Identifying and Rewriting Internalized Beliefs

Many of the beliefs we hold about ourselves were handed to us, not chosen. They might come from childhood experiences, societal messages, or moments of rejection that left a lasting scar. To reframe your narrative, start by identifying these beliefs and challenging them:

1. **Spot the Beliefs:** Reflect on the negative things you say to yourself. Do you tell yourself you're "not enough"? That you have to work harder to be worthy? That people will

reject you if they see the real you? Write these beliefs down.

2. **Ask Where They Came From:** For each belief, ask yourself: *Whose voice is this? Where did I learn this?* Often, these beliefs originate from external sources—parents, peers, or societal expectations. Recognizing that they're not *your* truth is the first step to letting them go.

3. **Rewrite the Story:** Replace each internalized belief with an empowering one. For example:

- Instead of "I'm too much," try "I am just the right amount for the right people."
- Instead of "I have to prove my worth," try "My worth is not up for debate."

Write these new beliefs where you can see them—on your phone, your mirror, or in a journal—and remind yourself of them daily.

Shifting from Shame-Based Thinking to Self-Acceptance

Shame tells you there's something wrong with who you are. Self-acceptance says, *I am enough as I am.* Moving from shame to self-acceptance is a process, but it starts with choosing compassion over criticism.

1. **Practice Self-Compassion:** When you catch yourself being critical, pause and ask, *What would I say to a friend in this situation?* Then, offer that same kindness to yourself.

2. **Stop the Comparisons:** Whether it's comparing yourself to straight peers, other gay men, or societal ideals, these comparisons only reinforce shame. Focus on your unique path instead.

3. **Embrace Your Humanity:** Everyone has flaws, struggles,

and insecurities—it's part of being human. Accepting this makes it easier to extend grace to yourself.

Shame thrives in silence, so share your struggles with someone you trust. Vulnerability often leads to connection, which is a powerful antidote to shame.

Recognizing Your Inherent Worth Outside of Accomplishments

In a culture that often equates worth with achievements, it's easy to believe you have to *do* something to be valuable. But your worth isn't tied to your resume, your appearance, or your social media followers—it's inherent.

1. **Reflect on Your Intrinsic Value:** Ask yourself, *If I stripped away all my accomplishments, what would still make me valuable?* Maybe it's your kindness, your humor, your resilience, or simply the fact that you exist.
2. **Celebrate Who You Are, Not Just What You Do:** Make a habit of appreciating your qualities—not just your successes. For example, instead of focusing on "I nailed that presentation," focus on "I brought creativity and heart to my work."
3. **Lean Into Being, Not Doing:** Spend time simply being yourself, without striving or performing. Whether that's sitting in nature, journaling, or spending time with people who love you as you are, these moments remind you that you don't have to *earn* your place in the world.

Stepping Into Your New Narrative

Reframing your narrative isn't about pretending everything is perfect—it's about seeing yourself through a lens of truth and compassion. You are not defined by your past, your mistakes, or what others think of you.

As you rewrite your story, you'll start to feel the weight of old beliefs lift. You'll begin to see yourself as whole, worthy, and capable of living authentically. And when you honor your inherent worth, you give others permission to do the same. This is the power of a new narrative—it doesn't just change how you see yourself; it changes how you show up in the world.

Challenging the Fraud Stories

Imposter syndrome thrives on the stories we tell ourselves— stories about not being good enough, not belonging, or being a fraud waiting to be exposed. But those stories aren't facts; they're fueled by distorted thinking patterns and a harsh inner critic. The good news? You can challenge these narratives and replace them with more empowering truths.

Understanding How Cognitive Distortions Fuel Imposter Syndrome

Cognitive distortions are the mental traps that twist how we see ourselves and the world. They're sneaky but powerful drivers of imposter syndrome. Common distortions include:

1. **All-or-Nothing Thinking:** "If I don't get everything right, I'm a total failure."
2. **Discounting the Positive:** "That success doesn't count—I just got lucky."

3. **Mind Reading:** "Everyone secretly thinks I'm not qualified."

4. **Catastrophizing:** "If I make a mistake, it'll ruin everything."

These patterns create a distorted lens through which you see yourself, magnifying doubt and diminishing your achievements. Recognizing these distortions is the first step toward breaking their hold.

Using Evidence-Based Strategies to Counter Negative Self-Talk

Once you identify the cognitive distortions fueling your fraud stories, you can actively challenge them. Try these strategies:

- **Fact-Check Your Thoughts:**
- When a negative thought arises, ask yourself, *What evidence supports this? What evidence contradicts it?*
- Example: Instead of "I'm not qualified for this role," remind yourself of your education, experience, and accomplishments that prove otherwise.
- **Reframe the Narrative:**
- Turn self-doubt into self-empowerment.
- Example: Replace "I'm not ready for this challenge" with "I may not know everything, but I'm capable of learning and growing."
- **Track Your Wins:**
- Keep a journal or list of your successes, big and small. When doubt creeps in, revisit this list to remind yourself of what you've achieved and the value you bring.
- **Adopt a Growth Mindset:**

- Instead of seeing mistakes as proof of inadequacy, view them as opportunities to learn.
- Example: "I didn't get it right this time, but I'm gaining skills and experience for next time."

Practicing Self-Compassion in Moments of Doubt

Doubt is inevitable, but how you respond to it makes all the difference. Practicing self-compassion can help you navigate moments of uncertainty with kindness instead of criticism.

- **Talk to Yourself Like a Friend:**
- Imagine your best friend is struggling with self-doubt. What would you say to them? Use that same supportive tone with yourself.
- Example: "It's okay to feel unsure right now. You're doing your best, and that's enough."
- **Acknowledge the Struggle Without Judgment:**
- Instead of berating yourself for feeling like a fraud, simply notice the feeling and name it: *I'm feeling insecure right now, and that's okay.*
- **Use Affirmations to Reframe Doubt:**
- Create a few mantras to ground yourself in moments of self-criticism. Examples:
- "I am enough, just as I am."
- "My worth isn't defined by my achievements."
- "Doubt doesn't mean I'm a fraud; it means I care."
- **Pause and Breathe:**
- When doubt feels overwhelming, take a few deep breaths. Use mindfulness to bring yourself back to the present, where most of your fears don't actually exist.

Reclaiming Your Story

Challenging the fraud stories is about stepping into your truth. It's about recognizing that self-doubt doesn't define you and that you're worthy, capable, and deserving of success.

Each time you counter a distorted thought, reframe a negative story, or treat yourself with compassion, you're rewriting your inner narrative. You're showing yourself that you don't have to be perfect to be worthy—and that living authentically starts with believing in yourself, even when it's hard.

Building Self-Trust

Trusting yourself is foundational to living authentically. When you can rely on your own intuition, decisions, and values, you stop looking outward for approval and start living in alignment with your truth. But for many of us, self-trust is something that needs to be rebuilt—one small, courageous step at a time.

Learning to Listen to and Honor Your Intuition

Your intuition is your inner compass, guiding you toward what feels true and right. But years of masking, people-pleasing, or striving for external validation can muffle that voice. Reconnecting with it takes practice:

1. **Create Quiet Space:** Your intuition speaks most clearly in moments of stillness. Spend time journaling, meditating, or simply sitting with your thoughts. Ask yourself: *What do I truly want? What feels right for me?*
2. **Notice Your Gut Reactions:** Pay attention to how your body responds to decisions or situations. Does something make

you feel light and excited, or tense and uneasy? These signals are often more honest than overthinking.

3. **Experiment with Trusting Yourself:** Start with small choices—what to wear, what to eat, or how to spend your free time. Instead of second-guessing, go with your first instinct and notice how it feels to honor it.

The more you tune into your intuition, the more confident you'll become in letting it guide you.

Taking Small, Bold Actions to Rebuild Confidence

Self-trust grows through action. Every time you take a step—even a small one—toward your truth, you prove to yourself that you're capable and resilient.

1. **Set Manageable Goals:** Choose one area of your life where you want to build trust. For example, speaking up in a meeting, expressing an opinion, or setting aside time for something you love.
2. **Celebrate Progress:** Each time you honor your intuition or take a bold action, celebrate it! These small wins compound over time, strengthening your belief in yourself.
3. **Reframe Mistakes as Growth:** Building self-trust doesn't mean never making mistakes. It means trusting that you can handle them. When something doesn't go as planned, ask yourself: *What can I learn from this?*

Confidence isn't about being fearless; it's about acting despite fear. Each small, brave step reinforces your trust in your ability to navigate life authentically.

The Role of Boundaries in Protecting Your Authentic Self

Boundaries are an essential part of self-trust. They signal to yourself and others that your time, energy, and emotions are valuable and worth protecting.

1. **Define What's Important to You:** Ask yourself: *What are my non-negotiables?* These might include how you're treated in relationships, how much work you take on, or how you spend your free time.

2. **Start Practicing "No" and "Yes" Authentically:** Saying "no" to what doesn't serve you creates space to say "yes" to what does. Practice honoring your boundaries by responding truthfully in situations where you might otherwise feel pressured to comply.

3. **Communicate Clearly:** When setting boundaries, be direct but kind. For example: "I need some alone time to recharge" or "I can't take on more work right now, but I can help later."

4. **Enforce Consistency:** Boundaries lose power if they're not maintained. The more consistent you are, the more you'll reinforce your own sense of worth and trust in yourself.

Setting and maintaining boundaries is a way of showing up for yourself. It's a declaration that you value your well-being enough to protect it.

A New Foundation of Trust

Rebuilding self-trust is a process, not a destination. It's about listening to your intuition, taking bold steps toward what feels true, and creating boundaries that honor your worth.

As you build this foundation, you'll notice a shift: you'll

second-guess yourself less, rely on others' opinions less, and feel more grounded in your decisions. Self-trust empowers you to navigate life authentically—knowing that, no matter what, you have your own back.

Chapter 5: Unlearning the Need for Permission

The Myth of Permission

For many of us, there's an unspoken belief that we need someone else's approval to take up space, make bold moves, or live authentically. It's a myth we've been taught by a world that values conformity and external validation. But the truth is, waiting for permission keeps you stuck, while claiming your own agency sets you free.

How Society Conditions Us to Seek External Approval

From a young age, we're taught to look outside ourselves for validation. Think about it:

- **In School:** We're praised for following the rules, earning gold stars, and meeting expectations.
- **At Home:** Love and approval can feel conditional, tied to good grades, good behavior, or fitting into the family mold.
- **In Society:** Media bombards us with messages about what's "acceptable," reinforcing rigid standards around beauty,

success, and identity.

For LGBTQ+ individuals, this conditioning is amplified. The pressure to conform to heteronormative expectations can leave you questioning your worth and seeking approval just to feel like you belong.

The result? You internalize the idea that your value is determined by others. You wait for signs—an award, a compliment, a nod of approval—to feel worthy.

Why Waiting for Validation Keeps You Stuck

When you wait for permission to live authentically, you're handing over your power.

1. **It Delays Action:** You might think, *I'll pursue that dream when people support me* or *I'll express my true self when it feels safe.* But waiting often turns into an indefinite pause.
2. **It Keeps You Playing Small:** Seeking validation means shaping yourself to fit what others expect, rather than stepping into your full potential.
3. **It Erodes Confidence:** The more you rely on external validation, the less you trust your own instincts and worth.

No one else can give you the green light to live your life. The permission you're waiting for doesn't exist—it's something only you can create for yourself.

Understanding the Power of Claiming Your Agency

Agency is your ability to act on your own behalf, to choose your path, and to stand firmly in your truth. When you stop waiting for validation and start claiming your power, incredible things happen:

1. **You Define Your Worth:** Instead of measuring your value by others' opinions, you anchor it in your own beliefs about who you are.
2. **You Take Ownership:** Claiming agency means deciding, *This is my life, and I get to live it my way.* It's a declaration that you are in charge.
3. **You Give Yourself Permission:** To dream big, take risks, and live authentically—without needing anyone else's approval.

How to Start Claiming Your Agency

1. **Affirm Your Right to Be Here:** Remind yourself daily: *I deserve to take up space just as I am.* This isn't arrogance; it's self-acceptance.
2. **Make Decisions for You:** The next time you're faced with a choice, ask yourself, *What do I want?* not *What will make others happy?* Practice listening to your desires and acting on them.
3. **Release the Need for Universal Approval:** Not everyone will understand or support your journey, and that's okay. Your authenticity will attract the people who truly see and value you.
4. **Take Bold Action:** Even small steps—wearing something that expresses your style, setting a boundary, or pursuing a passion—signal to yourself that you're in control of your life.

Living Without Permission

When you stop waiting for others to validate you, you step into a new kind of freedom—the freedom to live unapologetically. Society might have conditioned you to seek approval, but you don't need it.

You already have everything you need to live authentically: your voice, your choices, and your inner power. The myth of permission loses its grip the moment you decide to claim your life as your own.

Letting Go of People-Pleasing

For many of us, people-pleasing feels like a survival strategy. Saying "yes" keeps the peace, avoids conflict, and ensures approval—or so it seems. But beneath the surface, constantly prioritizing others comes at a steep price. Letting go of people-pleasing is about reclaiming your time, energy, and self-worth so you can show up authentically for yourself and others.

The Hidden Costs of Always Saying "Yes"

On the surface, people-pleasing might seem like kindness or generosity. But when it becomes a pattern, it often leads to:

1. **Burnout:** Constantly meeting others' needs leaves little energy for your own goals, passions, or well-being.
2. **Resentment:** Saying "yes" when you mean "no" builds frustration, which can damage relationships over time.
3. **Loss of Self-Identity:** When you're always accommodat-

ing others, it's easy to lose sight of what *you* want or value.

People-pleasing doesn't guarantee acceptance or appreciation—it just ensures that your needs stay on the back burner.

How to Recognize When You're Over-Prioritizing Others' Needs

Breaking free from people-pleasing starts with awareness. Here are some signs that you might be putting others first at your own expense:

1. **You Avoid Conflict at All Costs:** Do you agree with others to keep the peace, even when you disagree?
2. **You Feel Guilty Saying "No":** Do you feel like turning someone down makes you selfish or mean?
3. **You Overextend Yourself:** Do you often take on more than you can handle because you're afraid to disappoint someone?
4. **You Seek Approval:** Do you base your self-worth on how much others like or need you?
5. **You Neglect Your Own Needs:** Do you regularly put aside your own desires, plans, or well-being to cater to others?

If any of this feels familiar, it's time to pause and ask: *Am I giving more to others than I'm giving to myself?*

Steps to Set Healthy Boundaries Without Guilt

Boundaries are not walls—they're guidelines that protect your time, energy, and emotional well-being. Setting them might feel uncomfortable at first, but it's a necessary step in letting go of people-pleasing.

- **Get Clear on Your Needs:** Spend time reflecting on what's important to you. What drains your energy? What restores it? Boundaries help you protect what matters most.
- **Start Small:** Practice saying "no" in low-stakes situations, like declining an invitation or rescheduling plans. Each time you honor your limits, it gets easier.
- **Use "I" Statements:** Communicate your boundaries in a way that feels firm but kind. For example:

Instead of "I can't help you," try, "I don't have the capacity to take this on right now."

Instead of "I don't want to go," try, "I need some time to recharge."

- **Release the Guilt:** Remind yourself that setting boundaries isn't selfish—it's self-respect. You can't pour from an empty cup, and honoring your needs allows you to show up for others in a healthier way.
- **Expect Pushback:** Not everyone will be thrilled when you start prioritizing yourself, especially if they're used to you always saying "yes." Stay firm, and remember that their discomfort doesn't mean you're doing something wrong.

Embracing a New Way of Being

Letting go of people-pleasing doesn't mean you stop being kind or caring—it means you stop sacrificing your authenticity to gain approval.

When you prioritize your own needs, you create space for relationships that are built on mutual respect and understanding. You'll feel lighter, freer, and more connected to your true self.

And the best part? The people who truly matter will respect and celebrate your boundaries, not question them.

You don't have to be everything to everyone. By saying "yes" to yourself, you'll discover the power of showing up as the real you.

Stepping into Self-Ownership

Self-ownership means recognizing that your life belongs to you—your decisions, your voice, and your worth are not up for negotiation. It's about stopping the search for permission, reclaiming your power, and standing strong in your truth, even when faced with criticism or judgment.

Identifying Where You're Still Waiting for Permission

Even when we consciously know we don't need others' approval, old habits of waiting for validation can linger. Ask yourself:

- **Where Am I Holding Back?**
- Are there dreams you've put on hold because you're afraid of what others might think?
- Do you avoid expressing opinions because you worry they'll be dismissed?
- **Who Am I Trying to Please?**
- Do certain people in your life make you feel like you need their blessing to move forward?
- Are you seeking approval from family, colleagues, or even

societal norms?
- **What Stories Are Holding Me Back?**
- Are you telling yourself that you're "not ready," "not good enough," or that others "know better"?
- These narratives often keep us stuck, waiting for permission that isn't coming.

Recognizing these patterns is the first step to breaking free.

Affirmations and Practices to Reclaim Your Voice

Your voice—your thoughts, feelings, and choices—deserves to be heard. To reclaim it, practice these steps:

- **Use Affirmations Daily:**
- Affirmations help rewire your self-talk. Here are some to try:
- "I am the author of my life."
- "My voice matters, and I trust it."
- "I do not need anyone's permission to be myself."
- Repeat these in the morning, before challenging situations, or whenever doubt creeps in.
- **Practice Speaking Up:**
- Start small. Share your opinions in safe spaces, even if they feel vulnerable. The more you speak your truth, the more confident you'll become in using your voice.
- **Reflect Through Journaling:**
- Write about times when you felt silenced or when you chose not to act because you were waiting for permission. Then, imagine how it would feel to take ownership in those moments.
- **Make One Bold Choice Every Day:**

- It doesn't have to be big. Wear something that expresses your personality, say "no" to something you don't want to do, or pursue a passion project.

Building Resilience to Criticism and Judgment

Stepping into self-ownership means not everyone will agree with your choices—and that's okay. Resilience allows you to stay grounded in your truth, even when faced with pushback.

- **Understand the Source of Criticism:**
- Often, criticism reflects others' fears or insecurities, not your worth. Ask yourself: *Is this feedback helpful, or is it about their perspective?*
- **Focus on Your Values:**
- Ground yourself in what matters to you. When your actions align with your values, external judgment loses its power.
- **Practice Detachment:**
- Not everyone will understand or support your journey, and that's not your responsibility. You're not here to meet others' expectations—you're here to live authentically.
- **Celebrate Your Wins:**
- Each time you choose self-ownership, take a moment to acknowledge it. Over time, these choices will build your confidence and reinforce your ability to handle criticism.

Stepping Fully Into Your Power

Self-ownership isn't a one-time decision—it's a practice. Each time you act from a place of authenticity rather than seeking approval, you're reclaiming your voice.

You have everything you need to chart your path and live your truth. Criticism and judgment may come, but they don't define you. By choosing self-ownership, you're stepping into your power—and there's nothing more liberating than that.

Chapter 6: Embracing Vulnerability

The Power of Being Seen

There's a unique kind of magic that happens when you allow yourself to truly be seen—not as a polished version of who you think you *should* be, but as your authentic, imperfect self. While it might feel terrifying at first, embracing vulnerability is the key to deeper connection, trust, and freedom.

How Vulnerability Builds Connection and Trust

Vulnerability is often misunderstood as weakness, but in truth, it's one of the bravest things you can do.

- **It Invites Authentic Relationships:**
- When you're open about your struggles, fears, and imperfections, you create space for others to do the same. This builds connections that are real, not based on facades.
- Think about the relationships that mean the most to you—they likely thrive on honesty and vulnerability, not perfection.
- **It Breaks Down Isolation:**

- Hiding behind a mask of "having it all together" can feel lonely. Letting others see you as you are reminds you that you're not alone in your experiences.
- **It Builds Trust:**
- When you show your true self, others feel safe to do the same. Vulnerability is a bridge to mutual trust and understanding.

Moving from Perfectionism to Authenticity

Perfectionism can feel like armor—if you appear flawless, you won't be judged or rejected. But the truth is, perfectionism doesn't protect you; it disconnects you.

- **The Myth of Flawlessness:**
- Perfection is impossible, yet striving for it keeps you stuck in a cycle of anxiety and burnout. It's also exhausting to maintain an image that doesn't reflect who you really are.
- Authenticity, on the other hand, is liberating. It's saying, "This is me, take it or leave it."
- **The Strength in Honesty:**
- Authenticity isn't about oversharing or being unfiltered— it's about aligning how you show up with who you truly are.
- When you move away from perfectionism, you give yourself permission to exist as a whole person, flaws and all.

Why Being Imperfect Is a Strength, Not a Weakness

Your imperfections are not shortcomings—they're what make you human, relatable, and resilient.

- **Imperfection Creates Connection:**

- People are drawn to realness. Sharing your struggles or quirks doesn't push others away—it draws them closer because they see themselves in you.
- **It Shows Courage:**
- Owning your imperfections requires bravery. It signals that you're confident enough in yourself to let go of the need to be perfect.
- **It Fuels Growth:**
- Mistakes and imperfections are where growth happens. When you embrace them, you open the door to learning, evolving, and becoming stronger.

Stepping Into the Light

Letting yourself be seen isn't about shouting your truths from the rooftops—it's about allowing yourself to exist fully, without apology. Vulnerability is your superpower, and imperfection is your ally.

When you stop striving for perfection and start embracing authenticity, you'll find that the connections you create are deeper, the weight you carry is lighter, and the life you live feels more aligned with who you really are.

There's power in being seen—not for who you're trying to be, but for who you truly are.

Overcoming Fear of Exposure

The fear of being exposed—of showing too much, being judged, or failing publicly—can feel paralyzing. It's a fear rooted in self-protection, but it often keeps you stuck, unable to fully embrace who you are or what you want. Overcoming this fear means understanding the difference between healthy privacy and hiding, managing the fear of rejection, and reframing vulnerability as a courageous act of self-expression.

Understanding the Difference Between Privacy and Hiding

It's natural to want to keep certain parts of your life private; not everything needs to be shared. But hiding is different—it's when fear drives you to suppress your authentic self or avoid situations where you might be seen.

- **Privacy is Intentional:**
- Privacy is about setting boundaries and protecting what feels sacred to you. It's a choice, not a reaction to fear.
- Example: Keeping a personal journal for yourself is privacy.
- **Hiding is Fear-Based:**
- Hiding comes from a place of shame or a desire to avoid judgment. It often means shrinking yourself to avoid risk.
- Example: Avoiding social situations because you're afraid of being judged is hiding.

Ask yourself: *Am I protecting something meaningful, or am I holding back out of fear?*

Techniques to Manage Fear of Rejection and Failure

Fear of rejection and failure is often rooted in a belief that these experiences will define your worth. Here's how to manage that fear:

- **Shift the Narrative About Rejection:**
- Rejection isn't a reflection of your value—it's simply a mismatch. Not everyone will understand or accept you, and that's okay.
- Try this mantra: *Their opinion doesn't define me.*
- **Redefine Failure:**
- Failure isn't the end—it's a step in the process of growth. Every stumble teaches you something valuable about resilience and persistence.
- Ask yourself: *What can I learn from this experience?*
- **Practice Gradual Exposure:**
- Start by taking small steps to share more of yourself in safe spaces. Over time, you'll build confidence and realize that vulnerability isn't as scary as it seems.
- **Breathe Through the Fear:**
- When fear feels overwhelming, use grounding techniques like deep breathing, meditation, or journaling to center yourself. Remind yourself that fear is temporary—it will pass.

Reframing Vulnerability as an Act of Courage

Vulnerability isn't weakness; it's bravery in action. It's choosing to show up fully, even when there's a risk of being misunderstood or judged.

- **Acknowledge the Strength in Vulnerability:**
- Sharing your true self takes courage. It shows that you're

willing to be real, even in the face of uncertainty.

- Vulnerability is also an act of trust—it invites others to see you as you are, not as a curated version of yourself.
- **Focus on Connection, Not Approval:**
- Vulnerability isn't about seeking validation; it's about creating opportunities for genuine connection. People are drawn to authenticity, not perfection.
- **Celebrate Acts of Courage:**
- Each time you allow yourself to be vulnerable, acknowledge your bravery. These moments, no matter how small, are proof of your strength.

Embracing the Light

Overcoming the fear of exposure isn't about becoming fearless—it's about learning to move forward despite the fear. When you stop hiding and start showing up authentically, you'll discover that rejection and failure don't define you.

Instead, they become stepping stones toward a fuller, freer life—one where vulnerability is no longer a threat but a testament to your courage.

Practical Steps to Open Up

Opening up doesn't have to be about sharing your deepest fears or struggles—it can also mean letting people see the parts of you that light up, like your passions, interests, and what excites you. Vulnerability is about letting others see the real you, step by step. By practicing small acts of openness, identifying safe spaces, and learning to ask for support, you can create deeper, more meaningful connections.

Exercises to Practice Small Acts of Vulnerability

- **Start with What Excites You:**
- Sharing what you're passionate about is a form of vulnerability. Whether it's a favorite hobby, a creative project, or a show you love, let others see what matters to you.
- Example: "I just started learning guitar, and even though I'm terrible at it, I'm having so much fun!"
- **Use "I Feel" and "I Love" Statements:**
- Practice expressing your emotions openly, not just about challenges but also about joy and excitement.
- Example: Instead of keeping quiet, try, "I felt really proud of myself for finishing that project," or, "I love how energized I feel when I'm hiking."
- **Journal and Share Selectively:**
- Write down thoughts, interests, or experiences you find meaningful. Choose one thing from your journal to share with someone you trust, even if it feels small.
- **Set a Vulnerability Goal:**
- Each day, aim to share something real about yourself—an interest, an emotion, or a personal story. Over time, these small acts of openness will feel more natural.

How to Identify Safe Spaces and People to Share With

Not everyone deserves access to your vulnerability, so it's important to choose wisely. Safe spaces and people make opening up feel easier and more rewarding.

- **Look for Empathy and Consistency:**
- Safe people listen without judgment, celebrate your interests, and respect your boundaries.
- Ask yourself: Who makes me feel energized or understood when I share something personal?
- **Test the Waters:**
- Start small by sharing something you're excited about, like a recent accomplishment or a new interest. Safe people will respond with enthusiasm and curiosity, not dismissiveness.
- **Notice Who Shares Back:**
- Vulnerability is reciprocal. People who share openly with you are often safe to share with in return.
- **Create Your Own Safe Space:**
- If you're unsure who to trust, join communities or groups centered on your interests or values. Whether it's an LGBTQ+ group or a book club, these spaces encourage authentic connection.

Learning to Ask for Help and Support

Asking for help is one of the most courageous acts of vulnerability, but it can also feel challenging. Here's how to make it easier:

- **Start with Simple Requests:**
- Begin with low-stakes asks, like advice on a project or help planning an event. This builds your comfort with leaning on others.
- **Be Clear About Your Needs:**

- Let people know exactly what you need. Specificity makes it easier for them to show up for you.
- Example: Instead of saying, "I'm overwhelmed," try, "I need someone to help me brainstorm solutions for this issue."
- **Embrace Support as Strength:**
- Asking for help doesn't mean you're weak—it means you value connection and trust others enough to let them in.
- **Celebrate the Connection:**
- Express gratitude when someone helps you or listens. It reinforces the bond and reminds you of the power of being seen and supported.

Vulnerability as a Path to Connection

Opening up isn't just about sharing your struggles—it's also about sharing your joys, passions, and quirks. Letting others see what excites you, what you care about, and what lights you up is just as meaningful as expressing your fears.

By practicing small acts of vulnerability, finding supportive spaces, and allowing yourself to lean on others, you'll discover that opening up isn't about exposing weakness. It's about building trust, creating deeper connections, and embracing the beauty of who you truly are.

Chapter 7: Finding Your Voice

What It Means to Speak Your Truth

Speaking your truth is one of the most empowering acts of self-expression. It's about being honest in how you communicate while staying grounded in empathy and self-awareness. It's not about being blunt or unfiltered but about ensuring that your words align with your values and intentions. Speaking your truth allows you to own your voice, set boundaries, and connect authentically with others.

Defining Authenticity in Your Communication

Authenticity in communication means expressing yourself in a way that reflects your true feelings, needs, and beliefs—without fear or pretense.

- **Speaking With Integrity:**
- Authenticity isn't about saying whatever comes to mind; it's about being honest and intentional.
- Example: Instead of agreeing to something you don't want to do, say, "I appreciate the offer, but it's not the right fit

for me right now."
- **Aligning Words and Actions:**
- Your truth isn't just in what you say but in how you live. When your words match your actions, you build trust in yourself and others.
- **Being Real Without Overexposure:**
- Authenticity doesn't mean sharing every thought or detail. It's about choosing what feels meaningful and true in the moment.

Balancing Honesty With Empathy

Being authentic doesn't mean disregarding how your words impact others. Balancing honesty with empathy helps you communicate your truth while fostering understanding and connection.

- **Speak From "I" Statements:**
- Instead of blaming or accusing, focus on how you feel.
- Example: Instead of saying, "You never listen to me," try, "I feel unheard when we talk, and I'd like us to work on that."
- **Consider Timing and Tone:**
- Speaking your truth is most effective when delivered with kindness and clarity. Pausing to consider your tone can turn difficult conversations into constructive ones.
- **Validate Others' Feelings:**
- You can be honest while still showing care for the other person's perspective.
- Example: "I hear that this is important to you, and I want to be honest about where I stand."

The Power of Saying "No" and "Yes" Intentionally

Authenticity in communication also means being deliberate about what you agree to and what you decline. Every "yes" and "no" should honor your needs and values.

- **Reclaiming Your "No":**
- Saying "no" can feel uncomfortable, but it's an act of self-respect. It sets boundaries and protects your energy.
- Example: "Thank you for thinking of me, but I have to decline to focus on other priorities."
- **Owning Your "Yes":**
- A meaningful "yes" should come from a place of genuine desire, not obligation. It allows you to engage fully with what matters to you.
- Example: "Yes, I'd love to help with that because it aligns with my goals."
- **Pause Before Responding:**
- When faced with a decision, take a moment to check in with yourself. Does this "yes" or "no" feel authentic?

Embracing the Freedom of Your Truth

Speaking your truth doesn't mean being perfect—it means being real. It's about showing up honestly, communicating with care, and saying "no" or "yes" in ways that reflect your true self.

When you commit to authentic communication, you create space for deeper connections, healthier boundaries, and a life that feels fully aligned with who you are. Speaking your truth isn't just about being heard—it's about living with intention and integrity.

Overcoming the Fear of Conflict

Conflict is often seen as something to avoid, especially if you've been conditioned to prioritize harmony over honesty. But conflict doesn't have to mean rejection or rupture—it can be an opportunity for growth, understanding, and even deeper connection. Learning to navigate disagreements without shrinking, staying grounded in difficult conversations, and reframing conflict as a normal part of relationships are key steps to overcoming the fear of it.

Strategies to Handle Disagreements Without Shrinking

- **Separate Yourself From the Outcome:**
- Focus on expressing your thoughts clearly rather than trying to control how the other person reacts.
- Example: Instead of retreating because you're afraid of upsetting someone, say, "I understand this might be hard to hear, but it's important to me to share how I feel."
- **Use "I" Statements:**
- Own your perspective instead of blaming the other person.
- Example: "I feel overwhelmed when plans change last minute, and I'd like us to work on communicating earlier."
- **Practice Assertiveness Without Aggression:**
- Assertiveness means standing firm in your truth while remaining respectful.
- Example: "I respect your perspective, but I don't agree, and here's why..."
- **Prepare Ahead for Key Conversations:**
- If you anticipate a disagreement, take time to rehearse your points. This can help you feel more confident and less

reactive.

How to Stay Grounded During Difficult Conversations

When tensions rise, it's easy to lose your footing emotionally. Staying grounded helps you maintain composure and communicate more effectively.

- **Regulate Your Breathing:**
- Deep breaths can calm your nervous system and keep you focused. Inhale for four counts, hold for four, and exhale for four.
- **Anchor Yourself in the Present:**
- Remind yourself: "This is one conversation, not a reflection of my worth." Visualize yourself as steady and unshakable, even if emotions run high.
- **Pause Before Reacting:**
- If emotions start to take over, it's okay to pause.
- Example: "I need a moment to gather my thoughts so I can respond clearly."
- **Focus on the Goal, Not Winning:**
- Approach the conversation with curiosity. Instead of aiming to "win," focus on understanding and being understood.

Understanding That Conflict Is Not Rejection

- **Conflict Is a Sign of Engagement:**
- Disagreements show that both parties care enough to address the issue rather than avoid it. It's a normal, even healthy, part of relationships.

- **Separate the Conflict From Your Identity:**
- A disagreement doesn't mean you're unworthy or unlikable—it's about the issue, not who you are.
- Example: Just because someone disagrees with your opinion doesn't mean they're rejecting you as a person.
- **Seek Resolution, Not Perfection:**
- It's okay if not every conflict ends with complete agreement. The goal is mutual respect, not uniformity.
- **Remind Yourself of Your Value:**
- Rejection, when it happens, doesn't define you. Your worth is not tied to someone else's approval or agreement.

Embracing Conflict as Growth

Overcoming the fear of conflict isn't about eliminating disagreements—it's about learning to navigate them with confidence and grace. When you stop shrinking or avoiding difficult conversations, you open the door to stronger, more authentic relationships.

Conflict isn't something to fear; it's something to approach with curiosity and courage. It's through these moments of challenge that you build resilience, deepen connections, and truly step into your power.

Building Confidence in Self-Expression

Confidence in self-expression is about more than just speaking up—it's about knowing your voice matters and learning to use it with clarity, assertiveness, and purpose. Whether in group settings, personal relationships, or at work, self-expression is a skill that can be strengthened with practice. By developing techniques to communicate assertively, advocating for your needs, and finding your voice in a variety of situations, you can show up authentically and powerfully.

Techniques to Practice Assertiveness and Clarity

- **Use "I" Statements to Express Your Needs:**
- Assertiveness starts with owning your feelings and desires without blaming others.
- Example: Instead of saying, "You always ignore me," say, "I feel unimportant when my input isn't acknowledged."
- **Practice Saying "No" and "Yes" Intentionally:**
- Saying "no" to what doesn't serve you and "yes" to what does builds confidence in your decision-making.
- Example: "I appreciate the offer, but I'm not available," or, "Yes, I'd love to be part of that project because it aligns with my goals."
- **Use Body Language to Reinforce Your Words:**
- Stand tall, make eye contact, and speak at a steady pace. Confident posture helps communicate clarity and conviction.
- **Start Small With Low-Stakes Situations:**
- Practice assertiveness in everyday interactions, like returning an incorrect coffee order or sharing an idea with a friend.

Exercises for Strengthening Your Voice in Group Settings

- **Prepare Ahead of Time:**
- If you're nervous about speaking in a group, jot down key

points you want to share. Having a clear structure can boost your confidence.
- **Use Positive Self-Talk:**
- Replace thoughts like "What if I sound stupid?" with affirmations like "My perspective is valuable, and it's okay to share it."
- **Start With Questions:**
- If speaking feels daunting, ease in by asking thoughtful questions to engage with the group. This shows your presence and builds confidence.
- **Practice in Safe Spaces:**
- Join a supportive group or community, like a workshop or club, where you can practice speaking up without fear of judgment.
- **Set a Small Goal for Each Interaction:**
- For example, commit to sharing one idea during a meeting or introducing yourself to someone new at an event.

How to Advocate for Yourself in Relationships and at Work

- **Know Your Non-Negotiables:**
- Identify your boundaries and values so you can advocate for them confidently.
- Example: In a relationship, say, "I need more communication around our plans to feel secure."
- **Frame Advocacy as Collaboration:**
- Position your requests as opportunities to work together.
- Example: "I'd like to take on more responsibility at work because I feel ready to grow. How can we make that happen?"

- **Practice Responding to Pushback:**
- Be ready to assert yourself if met with resistance. Stay calm and reiterate your needs.
- Example: "I hear your concerns, but this is important to me, and I'd like us to find a solution that works for both of us."
- **Celebrate Small Wins:**
- Acknowledge every step you take to advocate for yourself, whether it's asking for a raise, setting a boundary, or voicing a concern.
- **Seek Support When Needed:**
- It's okay to ask a trusted friend, mentor, or therapist for guidance as you navigate self-advocacy.

Owning Your Voice

Building confidence in self-expression takes time, but every small step reinforces your ability to show up authentically. By practicing assertiveness, strengthening your presence in group settings, and advocating for yourself in personal and professional spaces, you'll begin to trust your voice as a tool for connection and empowerment.

Your voice is powerful—it's not just how you communicate but how you claim your space in the world. As you learn to express yourself with confidence, you'll find freedom in knowing that your truth deserves to be heard.

Chapter 8: Living Fully and Unapologetically

What It Means to Take Up Space

Taking up space is about embracing the full weight of your presence and rejecting the idea that you're "too much." For too long, many of us have been conditioned to shrink, to fit neatly into others' expectations, and to avoid standing out. But taking up space means recognizing your value, owning your right to be seen and heard, and reclaiming the joy and playfulness that make life vibrant.

Challenging the Idea That You're "Too Much"

- **Deconstructing the "Too Much" Narrative:**
- The idea of being "too much" often stems from societal norms that police individuality and difference.
- If you've been told you're "too loud," "too emotional," or "too bold," know that these criticisms often reflect discomfort in others, not flaws in you.
- **Embracing Your Fullness:**

- You're not "too much"—you're enough. Taking up space means allowing yourself to express your emotions, opinions, and personality without apology.
- Example: Instead of dimming your excitement, lean into it. Let yourself be passionate about what matters to you.
- **Redefining "Enoughness":**
- Being "enough" doesn't mean being perfect or pleasing everyone. It means being authentic and allowing yourself to exist as you are.

Recognizing the Value of Your Presence in Any Room

- **Your Voice Matters:**
- Whether you're in a meeting, a social gathering, or a relationship, your perspective adds value. No one else can bring the unique combination of your experiences, insights, and energy.
- **Reframing Self-Doubt as Opportunity:**
- When you feel small or out of place, remind yourself that your presence is purposeful. You belong in every space you enter.
- Example: If you catch yourself thinking, "I shouldn't be here," reframe it to, "I have something meaningful to contribute."
- **Claiming Your Right to Be Seen:**
- Taking up space doesn't mean dominating others—it means showing up fully and unapologetically.

Reclaiming Joy and Playfulness as Acts of Resistance

- **Finding Freedom in Joy:**
- In a world that often demands conformity, finding joy in being yourself is revolutionary. Allow yourself to laugh loudly, celebrate small victories, and explore what makes you happy.
- **Rediscovering Playfulness:**
- Play isn't just for children—it's a vital part of creativity and self-expression. Dance in your living room, wear the outfit that makes you feel amazing, or dive into a hobby just because it excites you.
- **Joy as a Form of Defiance:**
- For LGBTQ+ people, embracing joy and playfulness can push back against the pressures to conform or downplay your identity. Reclaiming your right to feel good is a statement of resilience and pride.

Living Fully in Your Space

Taking up space means rejecting the lie that you need to shrink to fit into others' expectations. It's about owning your value, letting yourself be seen, and embracing the joy that comes with living authentically.

Every time you show up fully, whether it's by sharing your ideas, laughing unapologetically, or being true to your emotions, you inspire others to do the same. Taking up space isn't just an act of self-love—it's a ripple that encourages the world to be more accepting, joyful, and free.

Creating a Life Aligned With Your Values

Living a life aligned with your values means stepping into a version of yourself that feels authentic, grounded, and fulfilling. It's about knowing what matters most, making intentional choices, and releasing what no longer fits. This process isn't always easy, but it's a powerful act of self-respect and a key to living fully and unapologetically.

Identifying What Matters Most to You

- **Reflect on Your Core Values:**
- Take time to identify what truly drives you. Is it connection, creativity, growth, honesty, or something else?
- Journaling Prompt: *What qualities or experiences make me feel most alive?*
- **Distinguish Your Values From Societal Expectations:**
- Sometimes, what we think we "should" value is shaped by external pressures. Listen to your inner voice, not the noise around you.
- Example: You might value adventure over stability, even if society says the latter is more acceptable.
- **Clarify Your Priorities:**
- Ask yourself: "What do I want my life to stand for?" and "Am I spending my time in ways that reflect that?"

Making Choices That Reflect Your Authentic Self

- **Use Your Values as a Compass:**
- When faced with decisions, ask: "Does this align with what

matters to me?"

- Example: If creativity is a core value, prioritize time for your art or hobbies, even if it means saying no to something else.
- **Learn to Say "Yes" Intentionally:**
- A true "yes" should feel expansive, not obligatory. Honor your boundaries by saying yes only when it aligns with your values.
- Example: Say yes to a friendship that supports your growth but no to commitments that drain your energy.
- **Take Small, Consistent Steps:**
- Aligning your life with your values doesn't require big, dramatic changes overnight. Focus on small daily actions that reflect your authentic self.

Letting Go of Relationships or Commitments That No Longer Serve You

- **Recognize When It's Time to Move On:**
- Relationships and commitments that feel draining, restrictive, or out of sync with your values may no longer serve you.
- **Release Without Guilt:**
- Letting go can be hard, especially if you've been conditioned to prioritize others' needs over your own. Remember, you're not abandoning anyone—you're choosing yourself.
- Example: Politely decline a recurring obligation that no longer feels aligned with your goals, or distance yourself from friendships that don't support your growth.
- **Make Space for What Feels Right:**
- Letting go creates room for connections and experiences

that align with your values. It's not just an ending—it's a beginning.

Living in Alignment

Creating a life that reflects your values is one of the most liberating and affirming things you can do. It's an ongoing process of listening to yourself, making intentional choices, and trusting that living authentically will bring you closer to the joy and fulfillment you deserve.

When your actions align with your values, you build a life that feels uniquely yours—a life where you don't just exist, but thrive.

Celebrating Your Uniqueness

Your uniqueness is your power. The things that make you different—the quirks, experiences, and perspectives that are yours alone—are not flaws to hide but gifts to celebrate. When you embrace your individuality, you don't just honor yourself; you also inspire others to do the same. Celebrating your uniqueness is about living boldly, sharing your truth, and being a beacon of authenticity and courage.

Embracing the Parts of Yourself That Make You Different

- **Shift the Narrative Around "Different":**
- Instead of seeing your differences as something to fix, view

them as a source of strength. Your unique traits, whether they're in how you think, love, or express yourself, are what make you stand out.

- **Reconnect With What Makes You, *You*:**
- What do you love about yourself? Is it your sense of humor, your passion for obscure topics, or your unconventional path in life? Celebrate those things unapologetically.
- Exercise: Write down three traits or experiences that make you unique, and reflect on how they've positively shaped your life.
- **Dare to Be Fully Seen:**
- Whether it's how you dress, the way you talk, or what you create, lean into self-expression. Being yourself loudly and proudly is an act of liberation.

Sharing Your Story to Inspire Others

- **Your Story Has Power:**
- The journey you've lived—your struggles, triumphs, and lessons—is a source of connection. Sharing it authentically can inspire others to embrace their own stories.
- **Be Open About Your Journey:**
- You don't have to have everything figured out to share your truth. People connect with honesty, not perfection.
- Example: Talk about how you've overcome challenges like imposter syndrome or learned to embrace your identity.
- **Create Ripples of Courage:**
- Every time you share your story, you give others permission to do the same. Your courage to be vulnerable can create a ripple effect of authenticity in your community.

Living as an Example of Authenticity and Courage

- **Lead By Being Yourself:**
- Authenticity isn't just about speaking your truth; it's about embodying it in how you live, love, and show up for yourself.
- **Show That Imperfection Is Beautiful:**
- You don't have to be flawless to inspire others. When you embrace your imperfections, you model that it's okay to be human.
- **Celebrate Others' Uniqueness, Too:**
- When you honor your own individuality, you naturally create space for others to celebrate theirs. Build a world where authenticity is not only accepted but celebrated.

Unleashing the Power of You

Celebrating your uniqueness is a radical act in a world that often pressures us to conform. By embracing what makes you different, sharing your journey, and living authentically, you not only find freedom for yourself but also give others the courage to do the same.

Your uniqueness is your gift to the world. When you celebrate it, you light the way for others to step into their own truth, creating a more vibrant and authentic world for everyone.

Chapter 9: Thriving in Relationships

Authenticity in Friendships

True friendships thrive on authenticity. When we let go of pretense and embrace honesty, we create deeper, more meaningful connections. Authentic friendships aren't about perfection—they're about showing up as your full self and allowing others to do the same. This section explores how to cultivate relationships rooted in trust, honesty, and mutual care.

Letting Go of Friendships Rooted in Pretense

- **Recognizing Surface-Level Friendships:**
- Friendships built on trying to fit in or masking your true self can feel exhausting. If you find yourself hiding parts of who you are to maintain a relationship, it may be time to reevaluate.
- Ask yourself: *Do I feel like I can truly be myself around this person?*
- **Releasing With Grace:**
- Letting go doesn't have to mean conflict or resentment. It's

okay to gently step back from relationships that no longer align with your values or where you don't feel fully accepted.

- Example: Gradually reduce time spent on connections that feel draining, and redirect your energy toward relationships that uplift you.
- **Making Space for What You Deserve:**
- When you let go of friendships rooted in pretense, you create room for relationships that celebrate your authenticity.

Building Deeper Connections Through Honesty

- **Start With Vulnerability:**
- Opening up about your feelings, struggles, and joys invites others to do the same. Vulnerability fosters trust and deepens connection.
- Example: Share a personal experience or thought instead of sticking to surface-level small talk.
- **Communicate Your Needs:**
- Authentic friendships grow when both people feel heard and understood. Be honest about what you need from the relationship, whether it's more support, quality time, or space.
- **Celebrate Each Other's Truths:**
- True friends accept and celebrate your individuality. When you honor each other's authenticity, your bond becomes stronger.

Recognizing and Nurturing Reciprocal Relationships

- **What Does Reciprocity Look Like?**
- Healthy friendships are built on mutual care, respect, and effort. Both people should feel valued and supported.
- **Evaluate the Balance:**
- Reflect on whether the relationship feels one-sided. Are you always the one initiating, giving, or compromising? If so, it might be time to discuss the imbalance or reassess the connection.
- **Invest in Mutual Growth:**
- Reciprocal friendships inspire both people to grow and thrive. Celebrate each other's successes, support each other in challenges, and nurture a shared sense of care and respect.

Thriving in Authentic Friendships

When you embrace authenticity in your friendships, you create relationships that feel fulfilling, safe, and joyful. Letting go of pretense, being honest, and prioritizing reciprocity allow you to build bonds that align with your values and enrich your life.

Authentic friendships don't just reflect who you are—they support who you're becoming. By surrounding yourself with people who see, accept, and love the real you, you create a community where everyone can shine.

Authenticity in Romantic Relationships

Authenticity is essential for building and sustaining healthy, fulfilling romantic relationships. It means letting go of patterns like codependency and perfectionism, allowing yourself to be fully seen, and fostering a connection based on mutual respect and understanding. Being authentic in love isn't just about sharing your fears or struggles—it's also about letting your partner in on the things that light you up and excite you.

Breaking Free From Patterns of Codependency or Perfectionism

- **Recognizing Codependency:**
- Codependency often arises from a fear of rejection or a need to feel validated by constantly meeting your partner's needs. It can lead to sacrificing your identity and values for the sake of the relationship.
- Example: Always saying yes to your partner's plans, even if it means neglecting your own interests or boundaries.
- **Releasing Perfectionism:**
- Perfectionism can make you feel like you need to hide your flaws or present an idealized version of yourself to be loved. This mindset creates emotional distance and prevents true intimacy.
- Reminder: Love is not about being flawless; it's about being real.
- **Steps to Break Free:**
- Develop self-awareness around these patterns by asking yourself: *Am I being honest about my needs, or am I afraid to rock the boat?*

- Practice small acts of self-assertion, like prioritizing your passions or setting boundaries.
- Seek support, such as therapy or trusted friends, to unpack deeper fears of rejection.

How to Show Up Fully in Love and Intimacy

- **Be Vulnerable in All Areas of Your Life:**
- Vulnerability isn't just about sharing your fears or insecurities. It's also about showing your excitement, your passions, and what makes you *you.* Letting your partner into your world creates a deeper, more authentic bond.
- Example: Share your love for a niche hobby, a creative project, or a dream you're working toward.
- **Communicate Your Needs Honestly:**
- Authentic love thrives on open communication. Be clear about what you need—whether it's emotional support, quality time, or encouragement for your interests.
- Tip: Use affirming "I" statements like, *"I feel connected when we spend time exploring new things together."*
- **Embrace Emotional and Physical Intimacy:**
- Intimacy grows when you let go of the need to control how your partner sees you. Show up as you are—messy, excited, or vulnerable—and focus on the joy of connection rather than the fear of judgment.

Creating Partnerships Based on Mutual Respect and Understanding

- **Respect Includes Celebrating Each Other's Passions:**
- A relationship rooted in mutual respect means making space for each other's individuality. When you honor your partner's interests and share your own, it deepens your connection.
- **Foster Equality:**
- Healthy relationships thrive on mutual effort and care. Avoid dynamics where one partner consistently gives more than the other. Instead, aim to uplift and support each other's growth.
- **Grow Together While Staying True to Yourselves:**
- A strong partnership is one where both individuals continue to evolve. Celebrate each other's successes and stand by one another during challenges while allowing space for individuality.

Thriving in Authentic Love

Being authentic in a romantic relationship isn't just about vulnerability—it's about joy, playfulness, and the courage to be fully yourself. When you share your fears, your dreams, your interests, and even your quirks, you create a space where real connection can thrive.

True love is built on seeing and accepting each other completely—not just in moments of struggle, but also in moments of excitement and passion. By breaking free from limiting patterns, showing up fully, and creating a foundation of mutual respect, you cultivate a relationship where love feels expansive and liberating.

When you embrace authenticity in love, you not only nurture a deeper bond with your partner but also strengthen your relationship with yourself.

Building Your Chosen Family

In a world where acceptance isn't always a given, the idea of a chosen family becomes a powerful anchor for authenticity and connection. Your chosen family consists of people who uplift you, accept you as you are, and celebrate your growth. It's a community that reinforces your truth, providing a space where you can thrive emotionally and spiritually. Let's explore how to attract and nurture these meaningful relationships and why celebrating chosen family is a vital part of living authentically.

The Power of Community in Reinforcing Your Authenticity

- **Authenticity Flourishes in Safe Spaces:**
- Being part of a supportive community allows you to show up without fear of judgment. It's easier to embrace your true self when surrounded by people who accept you unconditionally.
- **Shared Values and Understanding:**
- A chosen family often shares your values, experiences, and goals. Whether it's the LGBTQ+ community or other supportive spaces, this shared understanding creates a foundation of trust and belonging.
- **The Ripple Effect of Authenticity:**
- When you surround yourself with people who honor their own authenticity, it inspires you to do the same. This

positive reinforcement strengthens your self-expression and self-worth.

How to Attract and Nurture Relationships With Like-Minded People

- **Start With Vulnerability:**
- Building authentic connections means letting yourself be seen. Share your interests, passions, and even your struggles—it's through vulnerability that deep relationships grow.
- **Seek Out Spaces That Align With Your Values:**
- Join groups or communities that reflect who you are, whether it's a local LGBTQ+ organization, a creative workshop, or an online group centered on shared interests.
- Tip: Don't be afraid to try new things; the right people often show up when you follow your passions.
- **Invest in Mutual Care and Effort:**
- Nurturing chosen family requires intention. Show up consistently, support others in their growth, and communicate openly to deepen bonds.
- **Be Selective and Intentional:**
- Authentic relationships thrive on quality, not quantity. Focus on building connections with people who genuinely see and accept you rather than trying to fit into groups that don't feel right.

Celebrating the Chosen Family Who Sees and Accepts You

- **Cherish the Connections That Feel Like Home:**
- Your chosen family is a reflection of the love and acceptance you deserve. Celebrate them for the joy and support they bring into your life.
- **Create Rituals of Gratitude:**
- Whether it's a weekly check-in, a shared tradition, or simply expressing your appreciation, take time to honor these relationships.
- **Build a Legacy of Love and Belonging:**
- The beauty of a chosen family is its ability to grow and evolve with you. By pouring love and authenticity into these relationships, you create a community that sustains and uplifts everyone involved.

Thriving With Your Chosen Family

Building your chosen family is one of the most powerful ways to live authentically. These relationships remind you that you are worthy of love and belonging just as you are. They provide a foundation of support and connection that strengthens your confidence and reinforces your truth.

Your chosen family isn't bound by blood—it's bound by mutual respect, shared joy, and unconditional acceptance. By investing in these connections, you create a space where you can fully thrive, celebrating not just who you are, but who you're becoming.

Chapter 10: The Practice of Authentic Living

Authenticity as a Daily Practice

Authenticity isn't a finish line you cross—it's a continuous journey of growth, self-discovery, and intentional choices. It's about showing up as your true self every day, even when it feels challenging or uncertain. By taking small, deliberate steps and staying mindful of your values, you can make authenticity a natural and empowering part of your life.

Why Authenticity Is a Journey, Not a Destination

- **You're Always Evolving:**
- Authenticity grows and shifts as you do. Who you are today might not be who you'll be in five years, and that's okay. The goal is to keep aligning with your truth as it evolves.
- Reminder: You don't have to have it all figured out. It's enough to take one step at a time.
- **Life Will Test Your Authenticity:**
- Challenges like fear of judgment, societal pressures, or mo-

ments of self-doubt are natural. Each one is an opportunity to choose authenticity again and again.

· Example: Speaking up in a meeting when it feels safer to stay silent.

· **Progress Over Perfection:**

· Authenticity doesn't mean being "perfectly real" all the time. It means striving to show up with honesty and integrity, even if it's messy or imperfect.

Small, Intentional Steps to Live in Alignment Each Day

· **Set Daily Intentions:**

· Start each morning by asking yourself: *What do I need today to feel aligned with my true self?* Whether it's prioritizing rest, expressing a boundary, or embracing joy, small actions make a big difference.

· **Practice Saying "Yes" and "No" With Intention:**

· When opportunities or requests come your way, pause and ask: *Does this align with my values?* Saying no to what doesn't serve you creates space for what truly does.

· **Celebrate Small Wins:**

· Acknowledge moments when you've chosen authenticity, no matter how small. Whether it's sharing your feelings, pursuing a passion, or simply wearing what makes you feel good, these choices matter.

The Role of Mindfulness in Staying Connected to Your Truth

· **Mindfulness Helps You Pause and Reflect:**

- Taking time to check in with yourself keeps you grounded in your values. Ask questions like: *Am I acting from fear, or am I honoring my truth?*
- Tip: Incorporate mindfulness practices like journaling, meditation, or a quiet walk to reconnect with yourself.
- **Respond, Don't React:**
- Mindfulness allows you to approach situations with clarity and intention rather than reacting out of habit. For example, before agreeing to a commitment, take a moment to consider if it aligns with what you truly want.
- **Stay Present in Your Choices:**
- Authenticity is rooted in the present moment. When you're mindful, you're more likely to act in alignment with your true self rather than defaulting to old patterns.

Thriving in Daily Authenticity

Living authentically doesn't happen overnight, nor does it mean you won't face challenges along the way. It's a daily practice of showing up for yourself with intention, courage, and self-compassion.

By taking small steps, staying mindful, and celebrating your progress, you strengthen your connection to your truth. Authenticity isn't about being perfect—it's about being present. And with each new day, you have the power to choose alignment, joy, and self-expression, one moment at a time.

Navigating Setbacks and Challenges

No matter how committed you are to living authentically, set-backs and challenges are inevitable. There will be days when doubt creeps in, when old patterns resurface, or when you feel like you've taken a step backward. These moments don't mean you've failed—they're opportunities to learn, grow, and strengthen your resilience. Let's explore how to navigate these challenges with grace and self-compassion.

How to Handle Moments of Doubt or Relapse Into Old Patterns

- **Recognize the Setback Without Judgment:**
- When you catch yourself slipping into old habits—whether it's people-pleasing, self-doubt, or hiding your truth—pause and take a breath. Acknowledge what's happening without criticizing yourself.
- Tip: Remind yourself, *This doesn't define me. It's just a moment, and I can choose differently moving forward.*
- **Reflect on the Trigger:**
- Ask yourself: *What caused me to revert to this pattern?* Identifying the root cause helps you address it more effectively in the future.
- Example: Did fear of rejection make you stay silent? Did perfectionism lead you to overwork?
- **Choose a Small, Aligned Action:**
- Even after a setback, you can make a conscious choice to move forward. It might be setting a boundary, speaking up, or simply reminding yourself of your progress.

Reframing "Failure" as a Necessary Part of Growth

- **Failure Is Feedback:**
- Instead of seeing setbacks as evidence of inadequacy, view them as valuable lessons. Each stumble shows you where you still have room to grow and refine your approach.
- Example: If an honest conversation didn't go as planned, consider what you learned about communication or boundaries.
- **Celebrate the Effort:**
- Trying and "failing" is still progress. It takes courage to step out of your comfort zone, and every attempt brings you closer to lasting change.
- Reminder: Authenticity is a practice, not a performance. Mistakes are part of the journey.
- **Embrace the Imperfection of Growth:**
- Growth is messy, non-linear, and full of surprises. Reframing "failure" as a stepping stone allows you to approach challenges with curiosity instead of fear.

Building Resilience for the Long Haul

- **Cultivate Self-Compassion:**
- Be gentle with yourself when setbacks happen. Speak to yourself as you would a close friend, offering encouragement and understanding instead of criticism.
- Affirmation: *I'm allowed to struggle, and I'm still worthy of love and respect.*
- **Lean on Your Support System:**
- Surround yourself with people who uplift and encourage

you. Whether it's a trusted friend, mentor, or chosen family, having a support system makes navigating challenges easier.

- Tip: Share your struggles with someone who can provide perspective and remind you of your progress.
- **Focus on the Big Picture:**
- Remind yourself why authenticity matters to you. When doubt arises, reconnect with your values and vision for the life you want to build.
- Practice gratitude for how far you've come, even if you're not where you want to be yet.

Thriving Through Setbacks

Setbacks and challenges are not signs of failure—they're proof that you're engaged in the work of growth and transformation. Each time you face doubt or an old habit, you're given an opportunity to practice resilience, self-compassion, and intentionality.

By reframing "failure" as part of the process and focusing on the lessons it brings, you build a stronger foundation for your authentic self. Remember, every step forward—even if it's small—moves you closer to the life you're meant to live. When challenges arise, lean into the journey, trust your progress, and keep choosing yourself, again and again.

Sustaining Your Growth

Authenticity is not a one-time achievement but a lifelong commitment to yourself. Sustaining your growth means cultivating habits and practices that keep you aligned, prioritizing your well-being, and remaining open to evolution. This section explores how to stay grounded, nurture yourself, and embrace continuous learning on your journey of self-discovery.

Identifying Practices and Habits That Keep You Grounded

- **Daily Check-Ins With Yourself:**
- Start each day by asking: *What do I need today to feel authentic?* This might be setting a boundary, pursuing a passion, or simply taking a moment to breathe.
- Tip: Use journaling, meditation, or a gratitude practice to reconnect with your values and intentions.
- **Create Rituals That Anchor You:**
- Whether it's a morning routine, a weekly hike, or time spent with loved ones, rituals help you stay connected to your authentic self.
- Example: A gratitude walk where you reflect on your growth and the moments you showed up fully as yourself.
- **Surround Yourself With Supportive People:**
- Your chosen family, friends, and communities play a big role in keeping you grounded. Build relationships with people who celebrate your authenticity and inspire your growth.

The Importance of Self-Care and Rest in Authenticity

- **Rest Is a Foundation for Authenticity:**
- It's impossible to show up as your best self when you're running on empty. Rest replenishes your energy, sharpens your focus, and gives you the emotional space to navigate challenges.
- Tip: Schedule rest as intentionally as you do work or social commitments.
- **Self-Care Is an Act of Resistance:**
- Taking care of yourself in a world that often demands constant output is a way to honor your worth. Whether it's setting boundaries or taking time for joy, self-care reinforces your value.
- **Prioritize What Nourishes You:**
- Self-care looks different for everyone. Find what recharges you, whether it's a creative hobby, quiet time alone, or connecting with loved ones.
- Reminder: Saying "no" to things that drain you is a powerful form of self-care.

Staying Open to Continued Evolution and Learning

- **Your Growth Doesn't Stop Here:**
- Authenticity is a journey, not a destination. Staying curious about yourself and the world keeps your growth alive.
- Practice: Reflect on your progress regularly and ask, *What's the next step in becoming more of who I am?*
- **Embrace Change With an Open Heart:**
- As you grow, your values, interests, and relationships may shift. Staying adaptable allows you to remain aligned with your evolving truth.

- **Seek Inspiration and Guidance:**
- Read books, attend workshops, or connect with mentors who can inspire and challenge you. Growth thrives when you're willing to learn from others and from new experiences.

Thriving in Sustained Authenticity

Sustaining your growth is about creating a life where authenticity feels natural and supported. By grounding yourself in meaningful habits, prioritizing rest and care, and embracing continuous evolution, you build a foundation that supports your true self every day.

Remember, there's no finish line to authenticity—just a series of moments where you choose to honor who you are. With each choice, you reinforce the life you're creating: one rooted in truth, connection, and joy. Keep going—you're worth it.

Conclusion: Breaking Free and Living Authentically

As we close this journey together, I want to honor the path you've taken. If you've made it this far, you've already shown courage and commitment to living a life of authenticity—a life where imposter syndrome no longer holds you back, and where being true to yourself is your daily reality.

This book was written with one goal in mind: to help gay men, like you, break free from the heavy weight of feeling like a fraud. You've explored the roots of imposter syndrome, challenged societal expectations, and taken steps to reclaim your voice and your worth. Now, let's reflect on how far you've come and look forward to the freedom that lies ahead.

Looking Back on Your Journey

When you started this book, you may have felt trapped by doubts about your worth or your place in the world. Perhaps you were hiding parts of yourself, striving for perfection, or shrinking to avoid rejection.

Through these pages, we've unpacked the stories you've been told—stories about who you should be and how you should live. We've uncovered the origins of imposter syndrome and examined the pressures of heteronormativity, societal expectations, and internalized shame. Together, we've begun to rewrite those stories and embrace the truth of who you are.

Acknowledging the Progress You've Made

Take a moment to recognize what you've accomplished. It's no small feat to face the deeply ingrained beliefs that keep you small. It takes immense courage to ask yourself tough questions, to let go of perfectionism, and to step into the world with vulnerability.

Whether you've started speaking your truth, set boundaries, or simply allowed yourself to dream of a life beyond imposter syndrome, you've taken powerful steps toward freedom. These actions are worth celebrating—they represent your commitment to yourself and your journey toward living authentically.

Living Authentically as a Gay Man

Breaking free from imposter syndrome means reclaiming your voice, your joy, and your sense of self-worth. It means rejecting the notion that you need to prove yourself to anyone. Living authentically as a gay man is about fully embracing who you are—your passions, your quirks, your values—and showing up in the world without apology.

Moving forward, authenticity will be a daily practice. It's in the small moments: choosing honesty over pretense, saying "no" to what doesn't align with your values, and giving yourself permission to simply *be*.

The Ripple Effect of Authenticity

When you live authentically, you not only change your own life—you inspire change in others. Your courage to break free from imposter syndrome sends a powerful message: that it's okay to be yourself, to take up space, and to live with pride.

Authenticity is contagious. It invites others to shed their own masks, to connect on a deeper level, and to embrace their truth. By living as your full, unapologetic self, you create a ripple effect that can transform friendships, relationships, communities, and beyond.

The Legacy of Living Authentically

The work you're doing now is bigger than just you. By breaking free from imposter syndrome and living authentically, you're contributing to a world where gay men—and all people—can feel seen, valued, and safe to be themselves. Your authenticity creates a legacy of empowerment, making it easier for others to follow your lead.

Imagine the impact of a community where every gay man felt confident, connected, and free to live their truth. That's the world you're helping to build with every step you take toward authenticity.

A Call to Action

As you move forward, remember: living authentically isn't a one-time decision; it's a lifelong commitment. There will be setbacks, moments of doubt, and challenges along the way, but you now have the tools to navigate them.

Keep choosing to show up as yourself every day. Keep speaking your truth, even when it feels vulnerable. Keep celebrating your uniqueness and honoring your worth. The world needs you—not a version of you watered down by fear or perfectionism, but the real you in all your complexity and brilliance.

If this book has helped you on your journey, I'd be honored if you shared your thoughts in a review on Amazon. Your feedback can help other gay men find this guide and begin their own journey toward authenticity.

Thank you for trusting me to walk this path with you. You are no longer defined by imposter syndrome. You are free to live your truth, to embrace your uniqueness, and to shine unapologetically.

This is your moment. Take it—and let the ripple effect of your authenticity change the world.

References

Coming Out in Adulthood: Combating Imposter Syndrome. (n.d.). Mental Health America. https://mhanational.org/lgbtq/comba tting-imposter-syndrome

Crosby, J. (2022, June 14). *What is queer imposter syndrome? Plus, how to cope.* Thriveworks. https://thriveworks.com/blog/ what-is-queer-imposter-syndrome-how-to-cope/

Deelen, M., & Deelen, M. (2024, August 9). *Queer imposter syndrome is real. Here's how people deal with it.* VICE. https://w ww.vice.com/en/article/queer-imposter-syndrome-interview s/

Fuchs, K. (2024, May 8). *What is LGBTQIA+ imposter syndrome?* therapist.com. https://therapist.com/identity/lgbtqia/lgbtqia-i mposter-syndrome/

JayAre, B. O. (2024, February 21). *You are enough: Queer imposter syndrome.* Feb. 21–27, 2024 | Real Change. https://ww w.realchangenews.org/news/2024/02/21/you-are-enough-que er-imposter-syndrome

Kahn, J. (2023, February 20). *Tips for Healing from Queer Impostor Syndrome — G&STC.* G&STC. https://www.gstherap ycenter.com/blog/tips-for-healing-from-queer-impostor-sy ndrome